P9-ARG-279

BREAKOUT BIOGRAPHIES

MISTY COPELAND

First African American Principal Ballerina for the American Ballet Theatre

Elizabeth Krajnik

PowerKiDS press

New York

Published in 2018 by The Rosen Publishing Group, Inc.
29 East 21st Street, New York, NY 10010

First Edition

Editor: Elizabeth Krajnik
Book Design: Tanya Dellaccio

Photo Credits: Cover Kris Connor/FilmMagic/Getty Images; p. 5 Rabbani and Solimene Photography/Getty Images Entertainment/Getty Images; pp. 7, 9 (bottom),13 (bottom) Hiroyuki Ito/Hulton Archive/Getty Images; p. 9 (top) Chelsea Lauren/WireImage/Getty Images; p. 11 (top) TIMOTHY A. CLARY/AFP/Getty Images; pp. 11 (bottom), 27 (top) Brad Barket/BET/Getty Images Entertainment/Getty Images; pp. 13 (top), 15 (top) Kevin Karzin/ASSOCIATED PRESS/AP Images; p. 15 (bottom) AFP/Getty Images; p. 17 (top) Paras Griffin/Getty Images Entertainment/Getty Images; p. 17 (bottom) Amanda Edwards/Getty Images Entertainment/Getty Images; p. 19 (top) The Washington Post/Getty Images; p. 19 (bottom) Patrick McMullan/Getty Images; p. 21 Andrew H. Walker/Getty Images Entertainment/Getty Images; p. 23 Kevin Mazur/WireImage/Getty Images; p. 25 Diane Bondareff/Invision for Barbie/AP Images; p. 27 (bottom) John Lamparski/Getty Images Entertainment/Getty Images; p. 29 (top) Pool/Getty Images News/Getty Images; p. 29 (bottom) James Devaney/Getty Images Entertainment/Getty Images.

Cataloging-in-Publication Data

Names: Krajnik, Elizabeth.
Title: Misty Copeland: first African American principal ballerina for the American Ballet Theatre / Elizabeth Krajnik.
Description: New York : PowerKids Press, 2018. | Series: Breakout biographies | Includes index.
Identifiers: LCCN ISBN 9781538326268 (pbk.) | ISBN 9781538325575 (library bound) | ISBN 9781538326275 (6 pack)
Subjects: LCSH: Copeland, Misty–Juvenile literature. | Ballet dancers–United States–Biography–Juvenile literature. | African American dancers–Biography–Juvenile literature.
Classification: LCC GV1785.C635 K73 2018 | DDC 792.8092 B–dc23

Manufactured in the United States of America

CPSIA Compliance Information: Batch #BW18PK For Further Information contact Rosen Publishing, New York, New York at 1-800-237-9932

CONTENTS

THE FIRST
AT ABT

American Ballet Theatre, or ABT, was founded in 1940 and has earned recognition as one of the greatest dance companies in the world. Since its founding, ABT has performed the best ballets from around the world and encourages **choreographers** to create new ballets.

George Balanchine, famous choreographer and cofounder of the New York City Ballet, described the ideal ballerina as having a small head, sloping shoulders, long legs, big feet, and a narrow rib cage. Copeland, however, has a curvy figure and has been told she's too muscular for classical ballet.

Most dancers in the United States' top ballet companies have been white. In June 2015, Copeland became the first African American woman to be promoted

In 2012, Copeland performed with ABT as the Firebird in Igor Stravinsky's *The Firebird*. Alexei Ratmansky created new choreography for the ballet.

A DIFFICULT
UPBRINGING

Misty Danielle Copeland was born on September 10, 1982, in Kansas City, Missouri. Her mother, Sylvia DelaCerna, has six children. Four of them—Erica, Doug Jr., Chris, and Misty—were born while DelaCerna was married to her second husband, Doug Copeland. When Misty was just two years old, her mother left Doug and moved the family to Bellflower, California.

In Bellflower, Copeland's mother began dating and eventually married Harold Brown, who was an alcoholic. Brown is the father of Copeland's half-sister Lindsey. Five years after they moved in with Brown, Copeland's family left again and moved to San Pedro, California. There, they moved in with Robert DelaCerna, their mother's fourth husband, who was emotionally and physically **abusive** to his wife and some of his stepchildren. DelaCerna is the father of Copeland's half-brother Cameron.

Even though Copeland's childhood was **unconventional**, she's broken the mold to become a successful ballet dancer.

THE
DRILL TEAM

While living in San Pedro, Copeland attended Dana Middle School. There, she tried out to be part of the drill team and follow in her sister Erica's footsteps. Drill teams perform dance routines, or a series of steps that are repeated as part of a performance.

Copeland performed a solo, or a performance done without another person, that she and Erica choreographed. Her solo impressed the drill team coach so much that she was made team captain. As captain, Copeland created choreography for the team and led team practices. Even though she was the smallest girl on the team, Copeland commanded her teammates' respect.

The drill team coach, Elizabeth Cantine, was trained in classical ballet. She noticed Copeland's ability to easily pick up choreography and had a brilliant idea.

ELIZABETH CANTINE

Cantine remained a part of Copeland's life well after she left Dana Middle School.

BOYS AND GIRLS CLUB BALLET

Cantine strongly encouraged Copeland to attend free ballet classes at the San Pedro Boys and Girls Club. There, Copeland and her siblings would wait after school for their mother to pick them up. Cindy Bradley, a friend of Cantine's, taught a basic ballet class there that focused on the fundamentals.

Copeland was 13 years old when she began her ballet training at the San Pedro Boys and Girls Club. She often doubted herself because of her age. Most ballet dancers begin their training when they're very young. Bradley was impressed by Copeland's grace, her flexibility, or ability to bend, and her ability to perform ballet moves early in her training.

Bradley had her own studio, the San Pedro Dance Center. She asked Copeland to continue her training in a more formal and **intensive** setting.

BALLET TERMS

Ballet originated in Italy, but it became an important part of the French royal court in the 17th century. Since then, the universal language of ballet has been French. The following are basic ballet terms:

corps de ballet: The group of dancers that make a complete unit in a ballet company.

en pointe: When a dancer stands on the tips of her toes while wearing special pointe shoes.

pas de deux: A dance for two people.

pirouette: A complete turn of the body on one foot.

plié: A bending of the knees outward by a ballet dancer with the back held straight.

EN POINTE

After just eight weeks of studying at the San Pedro Dance Center, Copeland stood en pointe for the first time. Copeland studied there for three years.

GETTING
NOTICED

During Copeland's first year at Bradley's studio, she danced the lead part of Clara in *The Nutcracker*. A year later, Copeland danced the lead part of Clare in a retelling of *The Nutcracker* called *The Chocolate Nutcracker*. At this point, Copeland was gaining media attention as a ballet **prodigy**.

Soon, Copeland entered ballet competitions to showcase her talent and be noticed by ballet companies. Her first competition was the **prestigious** Spotlight Awards. Copeland performed the role of Kitri from *Don Quixote*.

After Copeland struggled while practicing for her performance, Bradley decided to rechoreograph it at the last minute to fit Copeland's needs. Although she was nervous, Copeland performed her routine perfectly. She won the top prize for ballet, which was $5,000. She was noticed by some of the top ballet companies in the country.

CUSTODY BATTLE

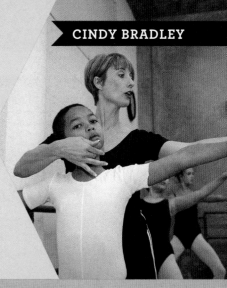

Not too long after Copeland started training at Bradley's studio, Copeland's mother, Sylvia DelaCerna, wanted her to quit ballet because it was too far away. Bradley asked DelaCerna if Misty could live with the Bradley family. Copeland's mother accepted. At that time, Copeland's family was living in a motel room. Copeland fit in well with the Bradley family, but her mother grew to disapprove of the arrangement. DelaCerna wanted her to live with her family again and, soon after, Copeland tried to become **emancipated** from her mother. This plan never worked out.

Don Quixote is just one of the many ballets Copeland has performed in with ABT.

GOING FAR FROM HOME

After her winning performance at the Spotlight Awards, Copeland was offered positions in the summer intensive programs hosted by the Joffrey Ballet and ABT. However, Bradley encouraged Copeland to audition, or try out, for as many summer intensives as possible. She also auditioned for the programs offered by Dance Theatre of Harlem, Pacific Northwest Ballet, and San Francisco Ballet.

Copeland was offered a spot in San Francisco Ballet's summer intensive program and accepted it. This was the first time Copeland had left home on her own. During that first summer intensive, Copeland realized that she wasn't as advanced as the other dancers. She had to work very hard to keep up with them.

When Copeland returned home, she began training at the Lauridsen Ballet Centre in Torrance, California, where she took ballet classes until 2000.

In 1999 and 2000, Copeland participated in ABT's summer intensive program on a full **scholarship**.

SUMMER INTENSIVES

Summer intensives are opportunities for young ballet dancers to work with and be noticed by some of the country's—and the world's—top ballet companies. Some dancers are chosen to attend these companies' schools year-round based upon their performance during the summer intensive program. In the ballet world, ABT is the top U.S. ballet company. Its foreign counterparts include the Paris Opera, Royal Ballet, and Bolshoi Ballet. Copeland received offers from all the programs she auditioned for except the New York City Ballet.

THE STUDIO COMPANY

Copeland was offered a place in ABT's Studio Company in 2000, following her second time in its summer intensive program. Before she began working with the Studio Company, she was an **apprentice** with the main company. Her apprenticeship required her to travel with the main company to China as a member of the corps de ballet. She performed in *La Bayadère*. This was Copeland's first move as a professional ballerina. She was just about to turn 18 years old.

When Copeland returned to the United States, she began working with the Studio Company. The Studio Company is made up of male and female dancers who work together in preparation for joining the main company. During her year as a member of the Studio Company, Copeland traveled throughout the United States.

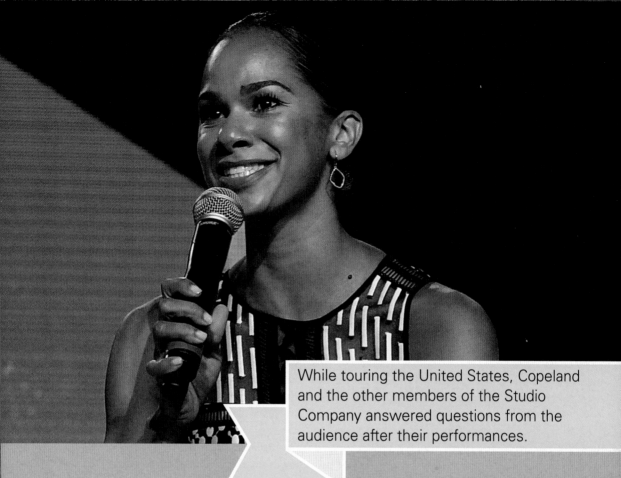

While touring the United States, Copeland and the other members of the Studio Company answered questions from the audience after their performances.

ABT'S SCHEDULE

ABT has two dancing seasons: spring and fall. In spring, ABT performs at the Metropolitan Opera House, or the Met, for eight weeks. In fall, ABT performs at the Koch Theater at Lincoln Center for three to four weeks. Sometimes ABT has a winter *Nutcracker* season that runs for three to four weeks at the Brooklyn Academy of Music. During the summer, dancers are given two months off, called "layoffs." Dancers work 35 weeks a year—18 weeks are spent **rehearsing** and 17 weeks are spent performing.

THE CORPS DE BALLET

When Copeland was just 19 years old, she was promoted to ABT's corps de ballet. ABT's corps de ballet is very competitive. Most of the dancers are trying to prove their talent and potential to the company's director to earn soloist roles. When she was promoted, Copeland was a new face to many of her fellow dancers and instructors. No one in the main company had heard of her before.

One day, while Copeland was working with a choreographer on a contemporary ballet, she hurt her back. She continued dancing in pain for a couple of weeks before she went to the doctor. The doctor told her she had a stress **fracture**. Copeland decided to take time off from dancing to heal and recover. For her first year in the corps, she didn't dance.

During her time as a corps member, Copeland struggled with her body type and feeling comfortable in her skin. ABT came to understand that her figure is part of who she is as a dancer.

BECOMING A SOLOIST

In 2007, Copeland was promoted to soloist at ABT. She had spent six years as a member of the corps de ballet and her hard work had finally paid off. At this point in her career, Copeland could see just how often ballet left out people of color. There were no other black women dancing for ABT, which left her feeling alone. However, she found comfort in forming meaningful relationships with other important people in the black dance community.

During her layoffs from ABT, Copeland worked with other ballet companies, such as the Dance Theatre of Harlem. She was able to perform principal roles with these companies, which helped her grow as a dancer. She has said that she was able to become a better dancer when she had time off from ABT.

Copeland was the first black female soloist at ABT in more than 20 years. The last black female soloist before her was Nora Koito Kimball-Mentzos.

DANCING WITH PRINCE

In 2009, while Copeland was a soloist with ABT, the singer Prince contacted her about dancing in the music video for his song "Crimson and Clover." She flew from New York City to Los Angeles to dance in his video. She created her own choreography and wore a one-of-a-kind dress.

Prince later contacted Copeland about touring with him in Europe. She traveled to Paris, France, where she was able to spend time with Prince and enjoy time off from ABT. On stage, Copeland made up a solo dance routine on the spot before Prince joined her.

Another year went by before Prince reached out to Copeland again. Together, they did a photo shoot for his upcoming American tour. Prince asked Copeland to perform at Madison Square Garden in New York City to kick off the tour.

During the shows performed on tour with Prince, Copeland wore the same one-of-a-kind dress that she wore in the "Crimson and Clover" music video.

PUSHING THE LIMIT

In 2011, ABT artistic director Kevin McKenzie pulled Copeland aside and told her she'd be learning the lead part in *The Firebird*. She assumed she'd be learning the part as an **understudy**. Copeland later learned that she would perform as the Firebird in the second cast of the ballet, making her the first black woman in history to perform the role for a major ballet company.

About six months before *The Firebird* debuted, or was performed for the public for the first time, at the Met, Copeland began to notice a nagging pain in her left shin. This time, however, Copeland didn't take care of her injury as quickly as she should have. She performed *The Firebird* in severe pain and, a few days later, she pulled out of the entire Met season. Copeland's doctor informed her that she'd need major surgery to fix the injury.

In May 2016, Mattel released a Barbie doll modeled after Copeland and wearing a costume similar to the one she wore for *The Firebird*. The doll is part of Barbie's Sheroes program, which celebrates female heroes.

LONG ROAD
TO RECOVERY

Copeland had surgery on October 10, 2012. After seven months of recovery, Copeland returned to the ABT stage. For those seven months, Copeland focused on healing. She took ballet class while lying on the floor so that no pressure was put on her shin, went to her doctor every three weeks to track her recovery, got massages and **acupuncture** treatments, and used machines to help her jump without straining her legs. She returned to rehearsing with ABT just five months after surgery.

Even though she had gone through major surgery, Copeland continued to push herself to be the best. In August 2015, her hard work was rewarded. She was promoted to principal dancer, making her the first African American female principal dancer in ABT's 75-year history.

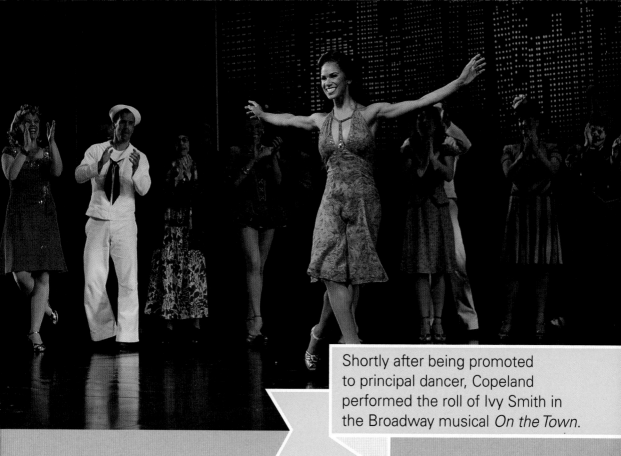

Shortly after being promoted to principal dancer, Copeland performed the roll of Ivy Smith in the Broadway musical *On the Town*.

OTHER ACCOMPLISHMENTS

Copeland is an incredibly accomplished woman. She has done **endorsements** for Under Armour, Dannon Oikos yogurt, Seiko watches, and the Boys and Girls Clubs of America. Copeland has been featured in commercials for Diet Dr Pepper, is a spokeswoman for Estée Lauder's "Modern Muse" perfume, and has been photographed by several famous photographers, including Gregg Delman and Annie Leibovitz. She has written three books: *Life in Motion: An Unlikely Ballerina, Firebird,* and *Ballerina Body: Dancing and Eating Your Way to a Leaner, Stronger, and More Graceful You.*

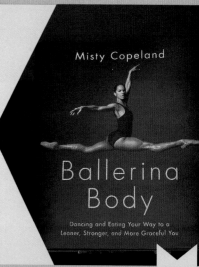

Misty Copeland

Ballerina Body

Dancing and Eating Your Way to a
Leaner, Stronger, and More Graceful You

WHAT THE FUTURE HOLDS

Copeland continues to fight for more **diversity** in ballet. Even though she has been a professional ballet dancer for more than 15 years, Copeland still sees racist comments on her social media posts. ABT and the Boys and Girls Club of America partnered to create Project Plié, a campaign that works to bring more diversity to ballet by training and supporting dancers of color around the country.

On July 31, 2016, Copeland married her boyfriend of more than 10 years, Olu Evans. They hope to start a family one day. In July 2017, Copeland was a guest judge on the TV show *World of Dance*. Copeland helped the other judges choose which dancer was the best of the best.

When asked what she'll do next, Copeland often responds, "Rehearsal." She isn't sure how much longer she'll continue dancing professionally, but she will most certainly

Copeland enjoys more than ballet. She and Evans attended a Golden State Warriors vs. New York Knicks basketball game on March 5, 2017.

TIMELINE

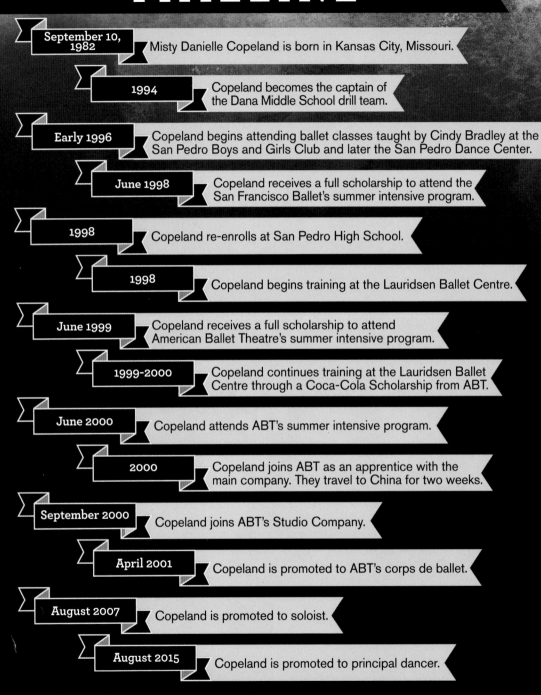

September 10, 1982 — Misty Danielle Copeland is born in Kansas City, Missouri.

1994 — Copeland becomes the captain of the Dana Middle School drill team.

Early 1996 — Copeland begins attending ballet classes taught by Cindy Bradley at the San Pedro Boys and Girls Club and later the San Pedro Dance Center.

June 1998 — Copeland receives a full scholarship to attend the San Francisco Ballet's summer intensive program.

1998 — Copeland re-enrolls at San Pedro High School.

1998 — Copeland begins training at the Lauridsen Ballet Centre.

June 1999 — Copeland receives a full scholarship to attend American Ballet Theatre's summer intensive program.

1999-2000 — Copeland continues training at the Lauridsen Ballet Centre through a Coca-Cola Scholarship from ABT.

June 2000 — Copeland attends ABT's summer intensive program.

2000 — Copeland joins ABT as an apprentice with the main company. They travel to China for two weeks.

September 2000 — Copeland joins ABT's Studio Company.

April 2001 — Copeland is promoted to ABT's corps de ballet.

August 2007 — Copeland is promoted to soloist.

August 2015 — Copeland is promoted to principal dancer.

GLOSSARY

abusive: Using physical violence or emotional cruelty.

acupuncture: A practice that may relieve pain by placing needles into a person's skin at particular points on the body.

apprentice: A person who learns a trade by working with a skilled person of that trade.

choreographer: A person who decides how a dancer or group of dancers should move during a performance.

diversity: The quality or state of having different types, forms, or ideas.

emancipate: To free someone from someone else's control or power.

endorsement: The act of publicly saying that you like or use a product or service in exchange for money.

fracture: A break, especially a broken bone.

intensive: Involving special effort, concentration, or work.

prestigious: Having importance or respect gained through success or excellence.

prodigy: A young person who is unusually talented in some way.

rehearse: To practice in private in preparation for a public performance.

scholarship: An amount of money a school or organization gives a student to help pay for the student's education and other expenses.

unconventional: Very different from the things that are used or accepted by most people.

understudy: A person who is prepared to take over another person's role if necessary.

INDEX

WEBSITES

Due to the changing nature of Internet links, PowerKids Press has developed an online list of websites related to the subject of this book. This site is updated regularly. Please use this link to access the list: